When in Doubt, Play Dead

LIFE ADVICE FROM AN
UNEXPECTED SOURCE

ALLY BURGUIERES

QUIRK BOOKS
PHILADELPHIA

Full Library of Congress Cataloging-in-Publication Data available upon request.

ISBN: 978-1-68369-384-0

Printed in China
Typeset in Avenir Next LT Pro, Cherry, Dreaming Outloud, and Rocking Horse

Designed by Paige Graff
Production management by John J. McGurk

Quirk Books
215 Church Street
Philadelphia, PA 19106
quirkbooks.com

10 9 8 7 6 5 4 3 2 1

TO ALL THE ANIMALS OF THE WORLD,
INCLUDING YOU

Contents

On perspective

A common misconception is that opossums have poor vision. But not only do opossums see the physical world remarkably well, they have a clear vision of making the most of what their world has to offer. Reject limiting misconceptions about your own abilities and embrace a uniquely opossum way of seeing the world!

When things seem upside down,
try going downside up.

The difference between a weed and a flower is often a matter of taste.

If you get on the wrong bus,
just get off at the next stop.

Repeat as necessary.

Eventually, you'll be exactly
where you need to be.

If someone calls you
a piece of work, say
"Yes! A masterpiece."

If someone calls you a handful, say "Thank you!" Handfuls are adorable.

Others might have prettier tails,
but yours may be more useful.

**

OPOSSUM TAILS ARE PREHENSILE, MEANING THAT
OPOSSUMS CAN USE THEM TO CARRY THINGS AND
HOLD ON TO BRANCHES WHILE CLIMBING.

Maybe you no longer have a tail. No cob, no prob!

***

THE TAILS OF ADULT OPOSSUMS RESEMBLE DRIED CORN COBS. LOSING A TAIL TO INJURY CAN MAJORLY IMPEDE AN OPOSSUM'S ABILITY TO THRIVE IN THE WILD. BUT OPOSSUMS—LIKE PEOPLE—HAVE A REMARKABLE ABILITY TO ADAPT AND SUCCEED THROUGH CHALLENGING CONDITIONS.

Others may be going faster or
farther than you. But your race is
unique—and you're the only one
in it. You literally cannot lose!

New perspectives bring
new adventures.

And new adventures
bring new perspectives.

***

ONCE LIMITED TO THE SOUTHERN UNITED STATES,
THE RANGE OF VIRGINIA OPOSSUMS HAS BEEN
STEADILY EXPANDING WESTWARD AND NORTHWARD.
THIS MEANS NEW PERSPECTIVES, NEW ADVENTURES,
AND NEW FRIENDS.

There's a whole world at night
that many others sleep through.

On appreciating yourself and your resilience

When appreciating the finer things in life, remember to include yourself. You're one of Mother Nature's best creations. Like the opossum, you're the result of millions of years of evolution that have prepared you to face today's challenges.

You've survived 100 percent of your problems so far. Great job! With that track record, you might even be immortal.

***

THE FIRST OPOSSUMS—AND THE FIRST CROCODILIAN
ANCESTORS—APPEARED DURING THE CRETACEOUS
PERIOD JUST AS THE DINOSAURS WENT EXTINCT.
WHO KNEW BEING CALLED A LIVING FOSSIL COULD
BE A COMPLIMENT!

Letting go is not the same as giving up.

Letting go might lead you to
something even better.

When in doubt, play dead.
Sometimes the best thing you
can do is nothing.

YOU OK?

YUP.

With enough time, most problems resolve themselves. Ask yourself, will this matter in five or even one hundred years?

***

OPOSSUMS ONLY LIVE FOR ABOUT THREE YEARS,
WHICH MEANS THEY HAVE EVEN LESS TIME THAN
MOST OF US TO WASTE ON STRESS AND DRAMA.

Go out on a limb—
that's where the fruit is.

Failure is part of life, too.
Embrace it!

So what if you didn't reach the top of the tree? That's OK. The view is pretty nice from where you are.

Who (and what) you are is
up to you and no one else.
Feel free to reinvent yourself
(daily if needed).

Let yourself be
wild and curious.

Chasing others' approval is exhausting because others can (and will) change what they approve of.

Approve of yourself and you'll feel a lot more secure!

Baddypants

Cutiepie

Know your best (and worst) angles.
But don't stress if people don't see
you the way you'd like them to.

Help others see the best in
themselves and you'll always
be beautiful to them.

Who you enjoy sleeping with is nobody's business.

***

OPOSSUMS CAN SOMETIMES BE FOUND
COHABITATING WITH OTHER ANIMALS
(OFTEN ARMADILLOS) WHO'VE ALREADY
DONE THE HARD WORK OF DIGGING A DEN.

And it's nobody's business
what's in your pouch.
Unless you've got snacks in there.
In which case, you should share.

Sometimes things crumble.
When you're ready, pick
another cookie and hope for
a better fortune.

49

On relationships

Opossums are often thought of as loners, but in fact, they demonstrate an enviable ability to coexist and even cooperate with others. Channel your inner opossum to enjoy a healthy approach to both socializing and solitude.

Friends come in
all shapes and sizes.

***

OPOSSUMS DON'T TYPICALLY POSE A THREAT TO
PETS. GIVE OPOSSUMS THEIR SPACE AND KEEP PETS
LEASHED OR INSIDE. COEXISTING WITH WILDLIFE
PEACEFULLY IS THE NAME OF THE GAME.

And weird friends
are the best kind.

(If you can't think of who
the weird friend in your group is,
it's probably you!)

You're never too big or too little
to hold hands (or tails).

Check in on your friends!

YOU OK?

Sometimes the best thing you can say is nothing. Just listen.

59

When help finds you, accept it!

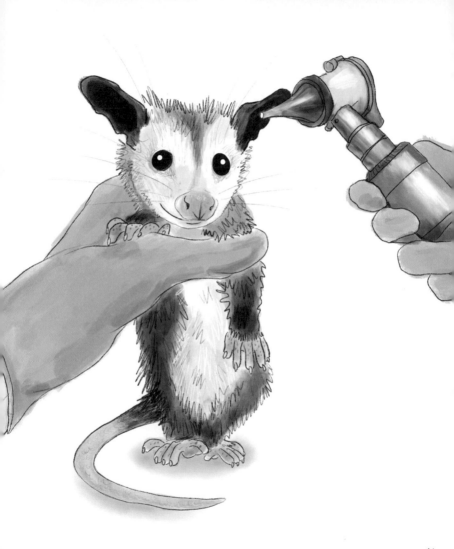

It's nice to carry each other.

But at some point, it's good to rely on ourselves. Otherwise, life would be opossums all the way down.

Expect nothing.
Accept everything.

(Except scam calls.
Don't accept those.)

CONGRATULATIONS!

YOU'VE WON 500 POUNDS OF BANANAS!

SAY "YES" TO ACCEPT!

Be forgiving of others;
it's the best way to ensure
your own faults will be forgiven.

You don't need to
go looking for love.
Love is all around you.
Sometimes literally.

***

MOTHER OPOSSUMS CAN NURSE UP
TO THIRTEEN BABIES. WHEN OLD ENOUGH
TO EXPLORE OUTSIDE THE POUCH, THE BABIES
RIDE ON THEIR MOM'S BACK.

On growth

Opossums, like alligators, experience indeterminate growth. Their bodies keep growing for as long as they're alive. Why stop when you can keep getting better with time?

It's OK to be
a late bloomer.

When the time is right,
you'll blossom.

And if not, that's OK.
Sometimes the coziest spot is
at the bottom of the pile.

Everyone is bad
at something.

Don't let that hold you back.
The trees would be empty if only
the best climbers climbed.

Let your creativity run wild.
Who cares whether it's "good"
or whether it's nonsense—
you'll have fun making things!
What you make might make
someone smile.

Try out a new language!

***

OPOSSUMS HAVE A REPERTOIRE OF NOISES THEY
USE TO COMMUNICATE AND EXPRESS THEMSELVES:
BABIES MAKE A SNEEZE-LIKE SOUND TO CALL TO
THEIR MOTHER. ADULTS LOOKING FOR A MATE MAKE
A STEADY CLICKING NOISE WITH THEIR MOUTHS.
A THREATENED OPOSSUM WILL OFTEN HISS AND
GROWL. AND FINALLY, SLEEPING OPOSSUMS
SOMETIMES SNORE.

You might make a new friend.

OINK?

Doing mental gymnastics
to hold on to an outdated
belief is a lot of work.

Save your energy for physical
gymnastics instead.

The best way to get what you want
from someone is to ask for it.
Nicely, of course.

Little things make big differences.

***

OPOSSUMS EAT DISEASE-CARRYING TICKS. THIS
MEANS EVEN THE SMALLEST OPOSSUM CAN CREATE
POSITIVE CHANGE FOR PEOPLE AND ECOSYSTEMS.

Let good things come to you!
It's OK to be an eager beaver,
but being a patient opossum will
bring you just as much magic in life.

Eat veggies!
Yours or someone else's—
it doesn't matter.

On fear, anxiety, and rough times

Everyone wants to throw in the towel sometimes. Breeze through difficult times like an opossum does—by harnessing an inner indifference, staying spicy when needed, and playing dead when all else fails.

When you feel a storm
approaching . . .

You can run toward the storm
like bison do, hoping to race
through it . . .

You can run away from
the storm like cows do,
trying (unsuccessfully)
to stay ahead of it . . .

Or you can save a lot of energy and run nowhere like opossums do, letting the storm pass over you.

We're all getting wet anyway.

Most fears are irrational.

rational

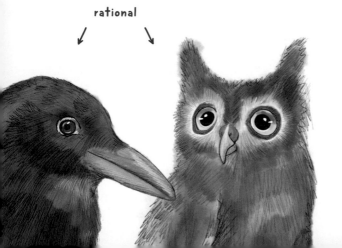

Some fears are rational.
It's good to know the difference.

rational

The fear of something is almost always worse than the thing itself.

EEP

Things are not always
what they seem.

Not an avocado.

Even happy days can be tough.
It's OK to wallow for a while.

WHY ME?

But don't become attached to your problems. If they're holding you back—or you're not having fun wallowing in them—let them go!

If you find yourself thinking of all the things that could go wrong, pause and ask yourself: What could go right?

On enjoying life

If you've ever stumbled upon a sleeping opossum, you'll know that few animals are as content, carefree, and comfortable as America's only marsupial. Let yourself bask in happiness at every possible moment. Then you'll truly be living the opossum way!

Enjoy sun puddles when
you find them.

And warm summer nights.

When winter comes,
you can snuggle then, too.

Smile! Unless someone tells you to, in which case you are well within your rights to scream.

Your smile is yours to share
when and if you choose!

Screaming can be fun
(as long as you don't make anyone
else feel bad by doing it).

Sometimes the darkest nights
make the brightest stars.

Be on the lookout
for hidden treasures.
The universe is bountiful.

FOUND ONE.

You're not too big or too small.
You're not too shy or too silly.
What you are is just right.

You're perfect.

Author's Note

IT WAS A MUGGY SUMMER EVENING WHEN I FIRST SAW THE BABY OPOSSUM I HAD AGREED TO HELP. I'D BEEN WARNED THAT OPOSSUMS WERE NOTORIOUSLY DIFFICULT TO REHAB; THEY'RE BOTH AMAZINGLY RESILIENT AND ABSURDLY FRAGILE. I SUSPECTED I WAS OUT OF MY DEPTH, BUT ANY DOUBTS ABOUT MY RESOLVE FADED WHEN I SAW THE MOONLIGHT GLINT OFF HIS ROUND, INKY-BLACK EYES. THE BABY, WHOM I NAMED SESAME, WRAPPED HIS LONG PINK TAIL AROUND MY FINGER, AND I WAS HOOKED. HE LOOKED AT ME WITH SUCH FAITH—SO PURE, TRUSTING, AND VULNERABLE—THAT I INSTANTLY KNEW I'D DO ANYTHING TO HELP HIM MEND. EVEN IN HIS SCRAWNY STATE, HE WAS PERFECT.

WITH THE AID OF LICENSED REHABBERS AND OTHER PROFESSIONALS, I LEARNED EVERYTHING I NEEDED TO KNOW TO CARE FOR HIM. I BOUGHT A MORTAR AND PESTLE AND SPENT HAZY MORNINGS GRINDING SUPPLEMENTS INTO POWDERS, MIXING THEM LIKE A MEDIEVAL ALCHEMIST. I FED HIM ORGANIC MEALS, CONSTRUCTED CLIMBING GYMS OUT OF BRANCHES, AND HAD MY SISTER CROCHET HIM A POUCH TO SLEEP IN. SESAME

WASN'T A CANDIDATE FOR RELEASE BACK INTO THE WILD, AND SOON, HE WAS FAMILY. MY SISTER VOLUNTEERED TO MAKE BIGGER POUCHES AND HAMMOCKS AS HE GREW. MY OTHER SISTERS (I HAVE FOUR) ASKED TO FACETIME WITH HIM INSTEAD OF ME. MY MOM AND DAD STARTED CHECKING IF THEIR GRANDBABY NEEDED ANYTHING FROM COSTCO. HE BECAME PART OF THE COMMUNITY, TOO. THE VENDORS AT THE FARMERS' MARKET WOULD ASK IF SESAME LIKED THEIR VEGGIES. ONE EVEN PRINTED A "SESAME APPROVED!" SIGN FOR HER STAND. AT THE LIBRARY BOOK SALE, THE LIBRARIAN PUT ASIDE A BOOK FOR SESAME CALLED *POSSUM LIVING*. INCIDENTALLY, IT'S NOT ABOUT OPOSSUMS, BUT THE SUBTITLE IS *HOW TO LIVE WELL WITHOUT A JOB AND WITH (ALMOST) NO MONEY*, SO IT APPLIED TO HIM ALL THE SAME.

LEARNING NEW SKILLS TO KEEP A STRANGE SPECIES OF ANIMAL ALIVE LEFT LITTLE TIME FOR STRESS. AND WHEN I DID START TO WORRY, IT FELT TRIVIAL. HERE WAS A BALL OF FUR THE SIZE OF A HAWAIIAN ROLL WHO HAD SUFFERED HYPOTHERMIA AND MALNUTRITION AND BEEN ALL ALONE IN THE WORLD, YET HE WOKE UP EVERY DAY (AND NIGHT) WITH A SMILE. HE DIDN'T REGRET THE PAST OR WORRY ABOUT THE FUTURE. HE DIDN'T

TURN DOWN HELP BECAUSE HE HAD BEEN HURT BEFORE. HE DIDN'T WORRY WHAT PEOPLE THOUGHT ABOUT HIM OR CARE THAT HIS HAIR WAS PATCHY IN SPOTS. HE BROUGHT PEOPLE TOGETHER AND GAVE THEM SOME EXTRA HAPPINESS IN THEIR DAY.

WHEN SESAME PASSED AT AN OLD AGE, HE LEFT BEHIND MANY FRIENDS AND FANS, AS WELL AS THE WISDOM OF HIS APPROACH TO LIFE. SOME OF THIS "POSSUM LIVING" WAS SPECIFIC ONLY TO HIM, BUT MANY PERSPECTIVES WERE CHARACTERISTIC OF OPOSSUMS AS A SPECIES. ONE OF MY FAVORITE QUOTES ABOUT OPOSSUMS IS "A POSSUM IS NOT LIKE ANYTHING ELSE UNDER THE SUN, EXCEPT ANOTHER POSSUM." SINCE HIS PASSING, SESAME HAS SENT ME COUNTLESS MORE OPOSSUMS—"SEEDLINGS"—WHO NEED HELP. I FIX THEM UP, AND THEY REVEAL SECRETS TO EMBRACING LIFE AND ENJOYING THE MOMENT. THEY TEACH ME AND THEIR FRIENDS ON SOCIAL MEDIA HOW TO BE MORE LIKE OPOSSUMS. WHEN THEY'RE RELEASED BACK TO THEIR WILD HABITATS, THEY LEAVE BEHIND A BIT OF CAREFREE CHEERFULNESS.

"ONE DAY YOU'LL HAVE TO EXPLAIN TO ME WHY YOU LIKE OPOSSUMS SO MUCH," MY FRIEND ANNIE ONCE SENT IN A MESSAGE, AFTER I BOMBARDED HER PHONE WITH PHOTOS OF

THE RESCUE OPOSSUMS IN MY CARE. THIS BOOK, I HOPE, ANSWERS HER QUESTION, AND YOURS, IF YOU FOUND YOURSELF WONDERING THE SAME THING. IN ADDITION TO REVEALING THE REASONS TO FALL IN LOVE WITH OPOSSUMS AND THEIR WAY OF LIFE, I HOPE THE PAGES IN THIS BOOK MAKE YOU SMILE AND GIVE YOU OPTIMISM, CONFIDENCE, AND A BIT OF WILD JOIE DE VIVRE. FINALLY, I HOPE THIS BOOK MAKES YOU HAPPY TO BE LIKE AN OPOSSUM—WHICH IS TO SAY: PERFECT, AND NOT QUITE LIKE ANYONE ELSE.

I FOUND AN OPOSSUM! NOW WHAT?

IS THE OPOSSUM INJURED?

IT'S DEAD

YES

NO

HOW BIG IS IT?

LONGER THAN EIGHT INCHES

SHORTER THAN EIGHT INCHES

IS IT ALONE?

THANK THE OPOSSUM GODS FOR BLESSING YOU WITH A HEALTHY OPOSSUM SIGHTING!

NO, MOM'S HERE! ALL IS WELL.

YES

1 2 3 4 5 6 7 8

DEFINITELY, 100%

ARE YOU SURE?
BETTER DOUBLE CHECK.

DOES THE OPOSSUM
HAVE A POUCH WITH
BABIES INSIDE?

NO

MAYBE NOT . . .

YES

R.I.P.

CONTACT YOUR NEAREST WILDLIFE
RESCUE AND REHAB CENTER!

FIND A DIRECTORY OF WILDLIFE RESCUES
AND REHABBERS AT AHNOW.ORG
(OR HEAD TO ITSMESESAME.COM/RESCUE
FOR MORE INFORMATION AND LINKS)

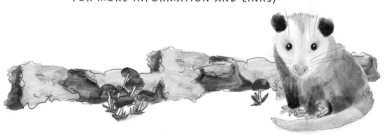

Acknowledgments

THANK YOU TO REBECCA GYLLENHAAL AND THE QUIRK BOOKS TEAM FOR BEING IDYLLIC COLLABORATORS AND BETTERING THIS BOOK IN EVERY WAY. I'D ALSO LIKE TO THANK MY AGENT, SORCHE FAIRBANK, FOR HER TALENT AND CREATIVITY, AND FOR BEING A FEARLESS ADVOCATE. I'M ESPECIALLY THANKFUL TO THE COMMUNITY OF OPOSSUM ENTHUSIASTS (VETERINARIANS, FELLOW REHABBERS, FOLLOWERS ON SOCIAL MEDIA), FOR COMPRISING ONE OF THE MOST CARING, EMPATHETIC, AND ENTERTAINING COMMUNITIES I'VE EVER HAD THE PLEASURE OF JOINING. COUNTLESS PEOPLE HAVE SUPPORTED OUR WORK AT SESAME THE OPOSSUM RESCUE, AND NONE OF THIS WOULD BE POSSIBLE WITHOUT THESE FRIENDS, FANS, AND PATRONS. TO MY FELLOW REHABBERS AND RESCUERS: COMPASSION FATIGUE IS REAL—THANK YOU FOR YOUR MORAL SUPPORT, AND I HOPE TO RETURN YOUR CARE AND ENCOURAGEMENT. THANK YOU TO MY FAMILY: JANICE, THOMAS, ELIZABETH, VICTORIA, GENEVIEVE, JULIETTE, ALICE, CALVIN, WENDY, AND BOBBY. TO THOSE WHO ENVISION A COMPASSIONATE FUTURE THROUGH ANIMAL RESCUE, VEGANISM, AND EVERYDAY KINDNESS, YOUR OPTIMISM AND PASSION MAKE ME PROUD TO BE PART OF YOUR RANKS.